a naked bone

a naked bone

mangaliso buzani

ISBN 978-0-9947104-6-8
ebook ISBN 978-0-9947104-7-5

Deep South
contact@deepsouth.co.za
www.deepsouth.co.za

Distributed in South Africa by
University of KwaZulu-Natal Press
www.ukznpress.co.za

Distributed worldwide by
African Books Collective
PO Box 721, Oxford, OX1 9EN, UK
www.africanbookscollective.com/publishers/deep-south

Deep South and the author acknowledge the financial assistance
of the National Arts Council for the production of this book

NATIONAL ARTS COUNCIL
OF SOUTH AFRICA

Earlier versions of some of these poems were published in
New Coin, Carapace, Aerial, South of Samora, and *Illuminations 32*
(special South African issue)

Cover design: Liz Gowans and Robert Berold
Text design and layout: Liz Gowans
Cover drawing: Amos Letsoalo 'Fisherman' (charcoal on paper)

Contents

I

II

III

IV

I

The rain

Straight to the garden
the rain came
wearing clear-beaded shoes
it landed on the naked seed
which was fast asleep on its bed
the first sound I heard with my ears
was the creaking of an old bed
that needed some missing screws
to tighten its legs
but the rain kept on falling
the bed kept on singing

My first lesson

I was dust
but after the work of the holy hands
I rose up like a wave of the sea
to praise the sky

on my arrival here
I looked at my hand
and I named it a hand
I kept on naming things
until a full body arrived

so I settled among the flowers
quiet as leaves
I was welcomed by the snails
who taught me how to make
a trail of light on a leaf

Death of the leaves

The sun
wearing a yellow robe
and silver shoes
touched the trees with fire
One by one leaves left their homes
falling without a word
light in weight but heavy with pain
They lost their green
their bones
their clothes
among the stones

Inside the river

Inside the heart of the river
I want to be a sea-dog
but this nose can't sniff
the scent of umamlambo

inside the head of the river
I want to be a writer
but this water
can't keep the paper dry

inside the shoes of the river
I want to walk like christ
but the floor of the river
can't keep up the weight of my feet

and I sink
to read poems
to frogs

The oven of god

Out of clay
from the oven of god
we came down here
losing our feathers
one by one

after each star
we left behind
to be human beings
we lost more of heaven

for sex in the garden
one foot on a thorn
brother
we must organise
some shoes

Revelation

From my palm
I blow away a pile of dust
that flies away with my flesh

for the first time on earth
my bones see my nose
and start to run away

I say to my aunts
the choir of god was here
wearing clothes of dust

they look at each other
and laugh

Imbawula

I want to build my house inside your heart, to give you pure purple love from the fires of my soul. I want to turn my bones to coal, wood and paraffin. I want to burn the imbawula for you, to make you roasted bread. I want to feed your tongue with words so that when you open your mouth you will spread the music of poems.

Naked in your fire

With your look
full of methylated spirits
you blaze my fire
burning from feet to head
I throw my clothes on the ground
made drunk by your beauty
I begin to promise my lips
now you will get a kiss

Dreams and bread

stones are piling inside my head
reminding me every day about my failures

last night they stabbed me many times
today I wake up bleeding from my ears
my stomach singing its chorus song

your dreams are not
going to put bread
on your table

Heaven

I'm told there are shelves in heaven
taller than the space between the ground and the sky
filled with papers from scrolls to books
all singing glory to god
there are no tables there
for drunkards to drink a beer

Since there will be no time to dance in heaven
let us make a table for the last supper
listen to jazz music
and find the time
to finish a bottle of wine

Kiss me

kiss me
touch my neck
go down to my sacred stick
which once moses used to hit the rock
pick the salt off my body with your tongue
our fire will cook love
and both of us will enjoy
god's special recipe

My daily bread

Far from the love of god
children armed with stones
surround me
they are sweating for hell
ready to lay down my bones
they dance about
patiently
to take the daily bread
away from my weary hands

With knives
longer than my arms
they are waiting for me
around a dark corner
I will meet my death
next to a spaza shop
where those who long for a piece of meat
will come out with onions
chicken soup
huge pots
to cook me
alive

Completely clean

Between the rails
that seem to touch each other in the distance
the man walks toward his dreams
too tired to open his eyes
he approaches his death
through the wheels of the train

at an instant
his body in two halves
his soul wearing new shoes
jumps over his bones
to reach for god

Themba

Themba my brother
sing your songs
the same christmas songs
we sang with combs
both before
a mirror

Themba
Themba
sing in me
use my tongue
I'll talk about
the strength of the worm
that ate your brain
and left you dangling on a rope

sing in me
I'll say whatever
in my last poem
that your body was full of earth

To my father

I have made the remains of you my home
among the falling bits of your dead body
your tendons have become my chewing gum

Your body a sea
has become a graveyard
that drips the fluid of the dead
that wakes me up wiping my face
to drink such water
salty from your pores
I hide under your ribs
it's raining under the ground

You feed me with rotten intestines
your half-rotten heart
lacks the flow of blood
which makes it as dust
softer than a brick

I have to follow your light
obey the commandments
of the ancestors
live among your bones
because you are more powerful than ever
much holier than yesterday

Prayer of a leaf

what if god has gone deaf
not to hear the simple prayer of a leaf
O dear god
turn my green tomatoes red

Seed of a lily

I bow to you seed of a lily
staring at your thighs under the water

take me to your world
where you feel no cold

I want to bath with you
listen to your quiet heart

II

Daily verse

On a dusty gravel road
a half naked child
walks towards a tree
which calls him by his name

Carrying an empty basket
listening from his singing stomach
he meets his sorrows
wrapped with thorns

On the shell of a passing snail
he reads his daily verse
Another 20 years to come
with nothing on the table

Ribs of a leaf

Perhaps I'm the only one
who breaks the frail ribs of a dry leaf
with a size seven shoe
the loud voice of my tiny toes
that disturb a tired ant
on a night shift
a bird who is trying to finish its duty
of counting leaves
my restless breath
that makes a spider
point a finger at me

I wonder
with this filthy heart
will I ever
enter eden again
or must I promise god
with a lot of long prayers
that repeat the same lines
god forgive me
help me throw away my last sin
and remain clean
next to your door

Leaves

Here in the windy town
I go up the stairs accompanied by dry leaves
I look at them as they crawl on the ground
wearing assorted camouflages
They are soldiers here
but nobody besides me
seems to get their attention
as they carpet the steps
I run to the library
and begin to read
A Rage in Harlem

Sick words

sick words are renting
the inside of my head
my soul has become a rude landlord
who always swears at my ears
scaring my bones saying
one day I will throw you outside

Dear doctor

There's something happening in my head
it feels like maggots eating up my brain
my disappearing brain
headaches today
tomorrow again

Dear doctor
don't send me away with a pain tablet
there's something happening inside my head
when winter comes I have to put it in an oven
when summer begins I have to put it in the fridge

The day he left

The old man hears a noise outside his house
kicks off the blankets with his wrinkled feet
and steps on the cold floor
Determined to cause chaos
he leaves his wife behind
begging him not to go outside
With hands of samson
he goes to war
Kneeling on the ground
he pulls igqudu lakhe from under the bed
to kill the intruder
The sound of thunder
doesn't lessen the strength of his mind
As if god is around
he walks in darkness
wearing no shoes
inside the kitchen
Before he switches the lights on
he falls on his back
crying for help for the last time on earth
He meets his death
among the pots
that have no hands
to help him

The moon has lost its light

I must find a way
to throw these heavy clothes away
that take so much money
out of my pockets
I'm tired of polishing my shoes
tired of my holed underwear
tired of pulling up the trouser
especially when I'm with you
tired of knotting a tie
that scares the garden away from me
the roll-on
that makes me smell sweeter

I feel like a toilet roll
I'm tired of my age
36 years with nothing
sounds like a song
they sing for me
when they lament
there's no life for a poet
god I pray
give me this day
my daily poems
I want no water
no butter
to catch me flies
for my dinner
god if you have lost
the art
of helping the poor
burn my bones
make me ashes

come down O my holy candle
I'm waiting for you in the garden
the moon has lost its light
and leads my one eye
to my grave
the other one to god
it is so hard
to cross this graveyard
without your candle light

I will be gone

Clouds wept
the sun wore a black gown
mourning beforehand
for my death
and I heard the footsteps
of my coffin
coming towards me

My poem begins here
so sick
wearing no clothes
it strolls down the road
to the graveyard
to tell the dead

I won't be here
this coming Saturday

    :::

Tomorrow I will be gone
hammered thin with stones
I will take only my soul with me
and leave dead meat behind

You will choose a coffin for me
a spaceship to heaven
where I will wait for you
planting flowers in the clouds
there I will open a door for you
where lovers sing for god

Since there are no chairs in heaven
I will leave my bones behind
for you to make a bridge
to reach god

:::

Out of options
to live another day
with my stomach close to my back
I will look to the earth
heartbroken

A pure voice
calls me
to come upon
a blunt knife
that has forgotten how to kill

I open a door
for my blood
to crawl on the ground
ears everywhere
drinking words

My soul
reads an obituary
for my bones
Manga
is no more

:::

Now that everything is over
I look at the river
no language
no science

the bones are no longer floating
the brain has suffered
the same blow

at last
my heart is shedding light
after each word I see god

Rain

Hit me rain
sit on the chair in my garden
and admire the legs of the moon
I want to show you my yellow shirt
which the banana has lent me
my green shoes
which a leaf gave me as a gift
my friend rain
I want to walk like nobody in the wind
bend to the left
bend to the right
and hold onto my black hat

The drowning heart

The ocean is deep
so is the wound of my soul
and I'm trapped here
inside a raindrop
I cannot swim
I have lost my legs
and all this has happened
in my heart too

Only then

Now with huge hands
of little flowers
I'm going to raise butterflies
let them drink from my dimples
keep them under my green armpits
away from the hands of the boys
until the girls come with their hair
then I'll tie them at the ends of their braids
so they don't leave the garden

Ear

A heart
has its language
the voice
of a drum
that's too difficult
for a soul
to understand

Ear
my only ear
do me a favour –
tell me what
my heart
is saying
to my soul

To my family

Today I will paint my house
with warm colours
I will paint the table
for six elbows
three chairs
for three bums
you will get your bowls
your spoons
I'll paint my love for you
your faces before my face
smiling
because you never smiled for me
always a sour sugar
always a sweet salt
a sadness I cannot tell

The fire

I want to write
the way the fire
recites its poems
cracking sounds of flame
for children to gather
and follow the light of my spirit

I want to hold a pen
look at the moon
let loose words on paper
like god throwing stars in the sky

III

A naked bone

I remind her about bananas, their weary yellow shoes,
apples with red-green-golden shirts, pears with huge
hips, pomegranates with bloody seeds. She smiles
and says to me, I used to bring you these when you
were young. I nod my head and continue to show her
a pumpkin with its yellow meat, cauliflower with its
pimpled face, a potato, a carrot, a beetroot, an onion
with its favourite all-weather jacket, all with muddy
shoes made for those muddy houses... mealies with
their hairy bodies which inspired God to come with
the hairy arms of Esau, all those who are not shy to
look the sun in its eyes: the slender sunflowers. She
smiles and says to me, I used to cook you all this
beauty when you were young... At this time she shows
signs of tiredness... she sleeps and I continue to remind
myself of her love.

:::

Tonight we are not going to sleep, we are going to
jump into bed with our shoes, and continue to walk
in our dreams. You on the paper writing poems, me
behind the paper reading poems. We will do this
together, exactly the way lovers make a baby together.

:::

I look above my head: a cloud cover. Before my eyes:
raindrops caressing the leaves. I rush to the taxi rank:
there's no space for my bums. The last taxi pulls off,
the rain falls on me on the way. And I step home,
completely a flower.

:::

Before a pen – a prayer: before a pen – a poem: before a pen – a song: before a pen – a story: Such energy: fire from a piece of paper.

:::

This is how we were made: two equal glasses of water to the sand and the sea: two waves singing a duet. Do you think the wind can separate us now?

:::

I want to stay awake. Let the birds that land on brows in search of dry twigs fly away. I want to watch you in this special night – touch your breasts until they become ostrich eggs in my hands.

:::

I kept on losing my smile: my hairs were thorns, I lost my movement like umga tree careful not to prick itself, I stood in the bush waiting for summer, for inxanxadi to feed me with a dry piece of meat.

:::

In this cold, I'm not going to let my little niece Kekeletso wet her clothes. In this wind, I'm not going to let her catch flu, let the hands of death pull her underground. I'll give her paintbrushes to paint her cold home with warm colours, so that she can lift the smile of God from the sad face of the earth.

:::

The wind is whistling, so wear as your scarf the arm of your lover round your neck: once more the bed brings closer the sweethearts to share one pillow. The wind sings, the bed sings, the song of the lovers.

:::

I continue to live wanting what I don't want. In the middle of the day, I throw down the pliers before my grandfather who is waiting for me to pull out his troublesome tooth: Grandfather, O grandfather, I don't want to be a dentist – go to the clinic.

:::

God's sticky hands that drip glue go on pasting each bone to another bone. We come into the world as body, a grape with its heart that pumps the wine, a soul that makes the drunkards feel even more holy than when they are sober. We live in such a sea, hard as seeds... people with their curiosity... from the choir of the vine... they pull one grape... they cut it... and then we are swimming in the sea of love... but this is not the end... we meet again inside the grape.

:::

Death is a street where all the lamplights are broken. There are no voices other than the sound of a cloud that is about to break into pieces of teardrops. The lightning, whose smile is just a fire. That's how you see your hole inside the skull of the soil.

:::

Under your blue face, your teardrops glide down my nose to reach my lips. How sweet your pure blood is, to touch my tongue with stories of heaven.

To feel you in me is to touch this world with my hand. Once more under a leaking roof that keeps my mouth open as long as the rain is falling. This drop, that drop: each drop that I catch with my mouth keeps my tongue tasting your soul.

:::

Today I'm face to face with death, I feel more drowsy than ever on earth. My eyebrows are heavy, I don't know when they gained so much weight. Because with these twin eyes I still want to see the light, exactly equal to the way my eyelids want to cover my eyes.

:::

A naked bone which is still thinking about what to wear for the day. A bone which has no shoes, an injured bone which recently lost its legs: the powerless child of an animal. Still they are standing to finish it with stones and hammers, to break into its holy house and steal its only life, its marrow.

:::

Flower, you give dignity to the garden. The sky weeps when it sees you, the stars refuse to close their eyes. The sun is in trouble, it can't go away forever, it keeps on coming back for its lover. Dust particles caress you

with their little hands which even microscopes cannot
see. Everyone wants to see you, you in your dress – the
colour. The light has made a plan to visit you, the light
during the day, the darkness at night, and I every time.

:::

I don't think it is too late. We can still be together in
this night. We can make the fire, see each other's faces.
The moon is high but its touch shines on us. We can't
play with that, it's too sacred to throw on the ground.

:::

Every day, wearing the clothes of a prickly pear, I
ask myself when I got these thorns that fly out of my
mouth every time I say a word. Is this the language
a poet should have on his tongue? To swear so much
that he disappears from anger?

:::

It's hell to work inside the room downstairs, there's
a ghost on the upper floor who doesn't sit down
and drink a cup of tea. Pacing the floor, he teaches
cupboards, chairs, tables, shelves, even the doors how
to tapdance on the floor.

:::

The world is a field of war. The pomegranate has come
with its soldiers still dripping blood, the cherry with
its red shirt still wet with blood, the strawberries with
their muddy shoes dirty with blood. Red is happy
when it claims the world as its own.

:::

I believe one drop of God's sweat can make one drunk, after his hard work of creating the world. You can feel from the fermented grape what made him drunk when He was creating the drunkards.

:::

Last night the rain was pouring cold tea into my cups. No guests complained, even the weeds smiled in the garden. We were drinking tea from heaven. I keep myself warm next to a loaf of bread. Every day I collect crumbs, and make muffins for my tongue.

:::

In my dream we were both chasing birds. You told me I eat words when I speak: I woke up preparing words to write.

:::

The hand is God. When you touch me I breathe. The river within me fills oceans with music. This heart sings – this soil sings – this mouth sings – these hands sing – these feet sing. You have given me life, in the month of September.

:::

The sky looks so sad today. I don't know why, whether it's because God is punishing angels in heaven or because of the sins we continue to caress with our holy hands. The sky is black, black like a crow on the crossbar of an electrical pole, sensing there will be some dead meat soon on its plate of tar.

:::

It was beautiful last night, I ran my fingers through your soul with my palm facing the ground. You were soft like flour, rough like salt crystals when water evaporates, when I was caressing your billion particles of dust and life. Earth, my only bed of soil – I just want to sleep on you, with my ear to the sound of your heart between your breasts.

:::

Just after I've finished cutting my nails, ants come close to where these fallen gravediggers remain for their funeral. Tricked by their shapes, they conclude "God has thrown down crescent moons". They carry them on their shoulders, for the time they will see the darkness again.

:::

The fig gets all its lessons from the weather. It goes through the university wearing a green gown. Through long lessons it gets the hips of a woman. The fig learns to master its walk while it is still hanging from the branch of a tree. Through the levels of the institution, it goes around wearing a red gown with a yellow hat, or a yellow gown with a red hat. But the life of the fig is for birds and human beings.

:::

Without thinking, I ate your fish. I put my hand into the sea, it came up with the fish into the air. The fish was begging for its life but I was too hungry to listen, I'm sorry. I threw it in the pan and fried it on the moon.

:::

I looked at the tree's face with my sad eyes. My lips were dried meat. It looked at me. Pity ran down its roots. It stretched out its arm full of fruit and threw into my cupped hands two guavas, my lunch for the day.

:::

When I enter through the door of my bed, the narrow hole of my blankets, the mood changes, my hands refuse to lean on the balconies, the four edges of the bed. Away from the eye of the lightbulb they remain under the blankets caressing my warm bums in search of a heater.

:::

My hair, you are everywhere in me: people say I'm hairy, and it's true. But they are blind to your beauty, my hair.

:::

Rose, tell me how is it to live inside my heart: how the bony burglar bars of my ribs have kept you safe from the pickers. I'm glad no tsotsi has ever seen you in that camouflage of blood.

:::

Under the belly of the dove, where soft feathers keep eggs warm, a saint is cooking – a small bird born from a floor of dry twigs that has never been scrubbed. But from that shack which gave it feathers, it sings of its love. I don't know why other eggs fell on the ground and chose to continue life rotting in the cold.

:::

A fig knows the truth. When a hand reveals a wedding ring, that's the end of its life on the tree. Faces with the eyes of children are shouting "mom we want jam." A fig Christ dies for the empty stomachs of the children, without lifting a stone.

:::

I'm scared: if the sun falls into a river, we will run out of water, the grass will become thorns, the trees will burn human beings with fire, cows will disappear. And so will we, if we can't kiss one another.

:::

A nest has only one room, no private room for meetings or lovers. It has no kitchen to cook mushrooms, no bathrooms to bathe the young. But it has a veranda to view the world from. A queen-sized bed of feathers and grass, it is full of music... for the pink feet of birds to dance on.

:::

The guava tree with its golden breasts looks more beautiful at night than the woman next to me. After a long waterfall of a pee I am tempted to touch it, but I stop myself. What would people say, seeing a shadow harvesting at night? I don't want to get the old lady into trouble and be accused of being igqwira.

:::

Feet are supposed to carry us to our graves, but we choose to close the doors, sit in our chairs, and wait for death. We produce nothing for God, not even a simple praise poem about how we love bread. We test new beds and give them wrinkles, hollows that we create with each beat of sex.

:::

It doesn't matter what they say about me. As long as you are here I'm fine. Come to me God: pull me by my nose. Turn me into a torch in the dark house of those who eat weeds for supper. Turn me into bread. Each stone you built me with is enough to bring back Christ. Make my words fishes so I can talk to starving children. Give me your word so I can give these poems wings to fetch more birds for your choir.

:::

With a whisper of the air, you make me open my eyes. I hold litres of bitter wine in the creases of my forehead. And you, who always touch my forehead with your lips, get drunk with my name, singing out Mangaliso, Mangaliso.

:::

My dog digging the ground says, this is our grave, we will sleep here together, this bone I'm hiding here is an anniversary for this day of master and dog.

:::

In the dark hole of the house the rat has become a landlord. I'm not ready to make you quiet with my howling stomach which sounds like a dying dog. I'm not ready to let your tongue taste the wine which is made of my teardrops and sweat. I'm not ready to throw two crumbs of bread on a broken piece of a plate... Wait a bit longer, my child, frozen in the hands of God. Tomorrow when the cows and sheep are playing in the fields, and chickens and pigeons are singing with small birds, I'll come for you. Open your little hands: see what you have brought for me from heaven.

:::

The stone has grown ears. At last I have someone to talk to. But the world is still quiet. The stone has no mouth to tell me its recipe for cooking fire when the cold winds seep through the house of the peasant, full of holes.

:::

The child went to his mother complaining about what wanted to come out of his stomach. She took a plastic bag and folded it beautifully, like a schoolkid off to school. The boy squatted as he was told, dropped one small mountain into the plastic. By the look on his face, he was at peace again with the world of God.

:::

I have never been happy in my life. With scars on my soul, I trace back footprints from my present size seven to the unknown size of my woollen baby shoes. I hold a meeting with the fig tree which once dislocated my elbow. I ask the rusted nail of the fence which once pulled me down by the turn-up of my trouser leg, why it broke my wrist in the middle of the night in my sleeping neighbourhood.

:::

My country – a graveyard with prison warders. A palace of skeletons wearing plastic clothes – the ill, the dying – manure for the garden of the president. On the table – a banana a lemon an orange a cabbage an onion without life.

:::

Little by little: maybe that's how I was made. The sand is piling up before my eyes, making sculptures from the hands of the wind – with shells for eyes. God, your breath goes a long way gathering particles to build lives. One breath, a thousand human beings; one blow, a thousand graves.

:::

After eighteen years of disappearance my father came to me with empty hands to say he wanted to be a father, to be a brother. Confused by what title to give him, I called him by his name, but he complained I was not respecting him. How hard to call him father, after so many rough years of living without one.

:::

I love my head with its disappearing M of hair close to my forehead. I wonder, my child, if you will carry the likeness of my hair on your head. If you'll be able to take the punches the balding man takes every day, his head that makes the whole world gossip that he's mad.

:::

Nwabisa Qhanqa, for you and me school life was far better than street life. We excelled with As if not Bs. They named you queen and me king. I don't know why we didn't put that into practice. Maybe I was blind then, or maybe you were. But now it is too late to comb your hair with my fingers – you are completely the soil.

:::

It is winter season: even the wind wants to reach for the lips of the moon, to caress its grey breasts. I want more blankets, you peel off the watermelon to cover me, until I disappear in your red world of brown-black seeds.

IV

She will come back

Sometimes I feel suffocated, the air that is supposed to hoist my head high puts the hand of death over my nose. When that happens I breathe with my eyes, and teardrops dry up and become stones. Mother, Mother, I feel alone.

:::

The bed had eaten her alive. Her power had been disappearing every day. The children were not aware she was on her way. So they played, jumping up and down on the mattress. Because every part of her body was painful, the jumping of the children made her swear very much, forgetting she was a Christian. For a while they'd stop, and then they would continue, because they were children, Nooi and Keke.

:::

I want to be like an apple, with its simple lines. I want to be in a gathering of those, deep-rooted in their customs, who scar their faces. I want to dance with an icecream-cone-shaped body like a weightlifter, for those who are sleeping under my feet, convinced God is around. I want to dangle from the branch of a flowering tree, totally an apple, from the hands of the one who brought me here, to tell the truth like a child who nurses his sorrows with an empty heart, who moans: My mother left me here alone, in this school of science and nature… No, no, the one who brought me here will never forget me in these chains. She will come back to take me home through the same hole that brought me here.

:::

If I had a choice I would have said to God: Father,
don't give me eyes: I'm not enjoying how people live
together. If I had a choice I would have said to God:
Father, don't give me ears: I'm not enjoying the gossip
that is roaming around.

:::

My mother is Lahliwe Teresa Buzani, umaChisana,
uNdebe, uKhophoyi, unKomoZibomvu, umaSithathu.
She left me in 2003 to roam the underground world. If
you see her, tell her uMangaliso her son was looking
for her, to share the white wings of a dove… we all
have to fly back home to the one who brought us here.

:::

I'm a suspect of what, I don't know. The bouncer
who gives tickets to get inside the tavern refuses me,
saying, "Not this one inside." My friend Kenneth says,
"This man doesn't even drink or smoke for God's
sake," but the bouncer pushes me aside. Here among
the drinkers, I become drowsy and depressed, maybe
because there are no shelves of books. Right there
before the door, I became dead, but the spirit of my
friends woke me up. My hair became overgrown, full
bearded, my fingernails became long. The shock of
death made people fear just by glancing at my face.

:::

With a knife longer than an adult's arm the boy took
out a piece of meat stuck between his teeth. Without

looking around him he spat it out of his mouth. The piece of meat flew away without wings, landing on the cheek of a reverend who was walking by. The furious reverend looked up and saw a big knife, and said "God forgive them," exactly like Jesus.

:::

Why we stay until we are thrown outside into the cold
    if not the rain
Why we choose to walk under the blind moon which
    enjoys its dark chair of clouds
Why we choose death instead of life
Why we make taverns our home
Sometimes I wish we could open the door of a tree
And stay wandering through its branches.

Mbizo Square

My second mother was Miss Dira from Kama Primary
School, she never raised a cane to me, only a black pen
over my pencil sketches. She loved me dearly, and
I loved her very much. I don't know how I lost her.
Growing up takes you to many places. Death puts an
end to our daily lives. She gave me two chickens to
start my family of chickens, I made their hok with old
boards. Magidi was always around to help me patch
the holes to keep the rats away. The chickens grew into
many. I had to be God, raise the knife of parting to cut
off their heads. I gave them food, they gave me eggs.
I gave them love, they gave me baby chicks – yellow
sunflowers with black seeds. That's how I got the name
uMfama, farmer.

:::

At school I was always wanted by the girls. It made me
scared because I didn't know what attracted butterflies
to a flower. I took advice from my mind, I covered my
nose with a dirty plaster, but the love letters didn't
stop.

:::

With words I wanted to build palaces, polish them
like my school shoes before I crossed Ferguson Road
to Johnson Marwanqa Higher Primary School. A
boy, I received love letters from Pumeza Tsoko. The
last letter was in English. Miss Tshagana got hold of
the letter somehow and told the class, "I wonder if
Mangaliso understands English, but don't you worry I
will translate into isiXhosa for you." The class listened,

and laughed at me. I listened embarrassed, but happy to be chosen by Pumeza from among all the boys in that class. From that experience I knew secrets come in many forms, on a candle flame sharp as a spear, on paper as a poem or a story. They come walking in front of our eyes to reduce us to dust.

:::

Mtshileli my schoolmate, you used to pick blackberries with me, I wish you were here to see how they have created wireless blackberries. I can't reach you there with a cell phone, but surely when I get there, I will make drawings of new technology designs. I will tell you how Johnson Marwanqa school closed down. There are no longer girls with blue uniforms and black berets on New Brighton Mbizo Square, the beautiful square which led us to our homes through Aggrey Road, Ngesi Street, Jolobe Street and Mendi Road. It is no longer the place where we used to gather, but a spot for amagintsa and mortuaries of cold bodies.

Sign language

The lead singer was Lahliwe, my mother, and Tukie
and Tonogo were the backup singers. They sang *Utloa
sefefo samoea*. We were their small congregation, we
clapped our hands, our grandmother hitting the side
of the wardrobe because we had no drum. We were
the ears to the singers. I wonder if they are still singing
together behind the moon.

:::

My grandmother fell inside the bathroom and hurt
her ribs. After that she abandoned speaking because
when she spoke a pain like a broken bone stabbed her.
That's why she chose to use sign language. We phoned
the ambulance, lucky it was near, it arrived within no
time. Because it was me who was looking after her,
I was sent with her in the ambulance to Livingstone
Hospital. She was not attended to, she suffered in that
hospital until she fell asleep. I went outside looking for
bread and juice, a diabetic patient mustn't go for long
hours without taking food. I woke her with bread, I
ate crumbs only with my eyes. I also suffered in that
hospital, there was nothing else in those 8 hours except
polishing chairs with our buttocks.

:::

It was very difficult to cross the doorframe of the room
with you grandma, without bending over to pick up
one of your teardrops with a tweezer. You were a
washing line made of bones, strange stiff clothes that
fluttered in the wind. Your wrinkled face that was
showing the last days of its beauty.

:::

The world had reduced you to dust, so in the space of
a minute the wind blew you away; hence the reverend
said dust to dust on your burial day. With a shovel,
six feet under the ground I have hidden you. Now
an invisible flower, you speak with me softly saying,
Manga, Manga, you are not alone, Ukhona uNyameka,
Nyameke is around.

The garden

Some are half bent, weeding the garden, deep in conversation with willow trees, while a carpet of geraniums sings. Others on the other side of the country are chewing hatred, in love with thorns, they hatch them like birds on eggs. I don't want to be like my neighbour – when he opens his mouth, splinters of thorns jump out to hurt the little hearts of a stalk of wheat grass.

::::

My friend tells me his story… just after his resignation he dreamed of bees and his ancestors… in these night visions they said he must slaughter a cow and grind sorghum seeds for umqombothi, because they were thirsty. Someone asked why he didn't dream of them while he was working. We keep quiet for the funeral of the last cents.

::::

Some stones turn to dust, trees grow tall, leaves fall on the ground and become human beings. Approaching winter, they surround themselves with walls, through the windows they wave a hand to me… In a winter like this one my hands refuse to come out of my pockets and wave back to my neighbours.

::::

I dip my toes into the mud, my whole body takes a new form. I become a bubble fish, swimming to the deepest ends of the world, to dance with other fishes.

:::

A rocking chair in the sea nods its head up and down. The sea asks, "Must I sing sea songs for you, must I recite poems of purple pebbles, must I give you sea food? Aren't you starving?" Yes, say the fishermen.

:::

This desert is dry, full of cactus plants that warn with thorny fingers everyone who comes close to them. I'm scared... this journey needs a dewdrop from the tongue of a generous leaf.

:::

Inside my head you are making a noise. Stop it, I can't even hear my heart. I don't want to hear about love anymore. Tell me stories, or at least read me a good poet of baked bread, who knows how to balance a pile of loaves on his head for the poor people.

:::

We had been talking life, fruit and vegetables. Now it was time to keep quiet, shuuuu... Ladies and gentlemen, it is time to throw down your bones. Someone has to fill the hole of this grave. In fear of stones and fire, we looked at each other wondering who was next.

The house was swept clean

Dead but still alive, I punched the lid of my coffin
up. The first particles of soil, small stones, dry
pieces of graveyard wood, had disturbed me in my
deepest sleep. They all started running when I said
my first sentence: "I'm not dead, this is my time to
write, take me back to my maroon chair from my
grandmother, to the cheap table my mother bought
for me…" The reverend threw his collar and garments
aside and ran, so did his congregation, my family,
my neighbourhood. I dusted off my body and threw
myself into a nearby river. I swam to the deepest places
of the river free from shoes, socks, shirt, tie, trousers
and underwear.

::::

Out of all the gifts we were given by God, I was given
a glass heart. Someone broke it, now it's bleeding. It's
cutting my flesh with its sharp pointed splinters. I keep
on dying a slow death.

::::

They sat the coffin behind the curtain between the
dining room and the kitchen. The mourners were there
to welcome the body of the deceased. The welcome
service started at 7am. Just after the reverend had
opened the bible to say a few words over the body, the
coffin shook itself very hard, as if it was saying No!
to the word of God. The curtain fell down, the coffin
continued to shake, making all the mourners run away.
The shocked daughter asked, What is happening in my
home? but the furniture had no mouth to say. And we

74

too, we had no answers for what had happened.
We concluded like all the locals, umamakhe betsiba,
her mother was a witch.

:::

On his death day he was much sadder than on his
birthday. His heart was a drumbeat. His eyes were
wide open, refusing to sink into the graves of his eye-
sockets. For the first time he took a broom, to take
over what he'd always told his wife was a woman's
job. Today he wanted to pause death as if nature was
a tape recorder. He took a feather duster, wiped off
all the spiderwebs, washed the dishes. Death kept on
knocking. He did a spring cleaning. The house was
super clean... death kept on calling... the man kept on
working... but death finally came in. He left his house,
his spoon, his chair, his bed, his television, everything
for another man, to use his cup for beer.

:::

Themba, you took your life before your eyes could
see the destruction we are seeing in this country...
everything fell down. I don't even know how I finished
this poem, because there's nothing left, not even me.

Wrapped with spinach leaves

Inside a taxi from Greenacres, off to Chetty with a
bunch of flowers to tighten the screws of our loose
affair. I'm about to call for the taxi driver to stop.
I see a white car dropping her off. Inside is a dark man
with a huge belly, who looks at her butternut bums
as she is walking away. The car makes a U-turn. It is a
smart car, not iphela, a taxi. I behave like a candle in
the dark. I make my first step into the house and find
them both in front of the TV, next to them the bones of
a braai. I greet them and go to the room for my clothes.
There is a towel on the bed for love games, which was
keen to tell me the news, but I heard nothing because
anger had already killed my sense of hearing. The bed
also tried to explain how they wet the sheets with their
sweat but it had no mouth to start or finish a single
sentence. I gave her her keys and made my way to the
open field, free from the chain of lies.

:::

He had placed a glass of wine on the table, destroying
her freedom to say no, in order to press her breasts. He
told her, "Today is your day I'm taking you away from
your man. You are leaving with me tonight…"

:::

I nearly died of heartache that Sunday morning.
Birdsongs disappeared, a dog barked when my heart
sang its songs of sorrow. Knock, knock at the door. Is
everything alright?

:::

At first the blows were hard – more than a tempest. I had to pack my clothes, cross the open muddy fields of Chetty. I had to leave my frustrations where I had picked them up, inside a pale blue house, the whole bad energy that nearly made my head explode. I had to be a tamed lion, because I loved her too much to raise a hand of anger to her face. I had to leave and go forth to find poetry that would never break my heart.

:::

I wish I knew her heart better, like a tomato, cut it in two halves, see its seeds – count them, plant them to give me tomatoes again… Then I would be happy to touch her red breasts, nod before a bloody towel and say she is in her periods of rose petals scattered everywhere on the bed. I wish I knew her heart…

:::

Maybe tomorrow I will cry. But not today, because all of my bones are yelling… to hell with her, to hell!

:::

Ever since I came back last Friday, I have been struggling to sleep, my heart heavy with thorns that gave me sleepless nights. But I was at peace yesterday. Andile bought me a small-sized cake to celebrate my birthday. It was decorated with a white spoon, feathers of a white dove. Today I woke up happy to find I slept tight. Now I'm listening to a choir of birds. The ghost of September that has been shaking me around one o'clock every morning has disappeared, even inside my head.

:::

Today is my last time with my bones, my rotting meat,
inflated bubblegum eyes, with this brain that makes
me think about how stones can grow horns and take
head-on all the bullies this world has ever produced.
I will never walk again beside a beautiful girl who
turned ugly on a Sunday morning. I will never worry
about the roses or packets of chips because I'll be a
potato under the ground myself.

:::

I thought I was going to forget her, but something
inside my heart brightens up, the candlelight of the
stone brings her before my eyes wrapped with spinach
leaves we used to eat together… because it is over and
we never had a chance to celebrate our last kiss. I give
you this poem as a token of love.

It is Thursday

Let's leave the stones alone. Let's speak of our fires.
Our miracles need our water… Close my mouth with
a kiss, I cannot stop talking about how I love you.
Concentrate on your miracle… Jesus went away with
his miracles. Turn me into a lover.

:::

There are children between our legs, some are soft,
some are hard, depending on how God designed them.
When we open our legs they fall. We smile, feeling like
mothers and fathers.

:::

That arrow of love that had travelled many countries
passed through my heart as well, leaving a hole, a
speaker, for soul music to take over my life. Soon after
that journey I absorbed the peace of the sea, I tasted the
holy teardrops of my gods, reminding me that always
God believes in love.

:::

Today after a long spell of heat, a few raindrops fell
in the garden. Plants have come back to life from their
dark houses, emerging to greet the morning and me
as well. I blow a whistle for a mealie sprout: it grows
taller than my height. I hum a tune for a rose: it shows
me red shoes. I recite a poem for a sunflower: it bows
at me with its massive moon face, throwing seeds
inside my mouth. We must be happy for these changes.
God is here for his reasons.

:::

The wind came down the road whistling an ancient song. It was dragging along stones, papers, huge boards, decayed tree trunks, dust, and glass splinters that can make you go blind forever. What else? Huge rocks of ice... Those were not the gifts we were waiting for, so we hid ourselves in our houses, praying for our rooftops not to be blown to the sea.

:::

After reading Pablo Neruda I went to the table to meet the paper head-on with a pen. I came out of that ink mess with fresh images that broke the legs of the table. I don't know whether it was the pressure of my hand pushing the pen down, or the power of the poems, but I didn't stop writing, and everything kept on tumbling down. I went down into a grave still writing. The bones there shook their fingers to say no, this is not the place for writing, it is a place to rest and guide those who are still alive. But the fingers broke, and I had to write about ancestors with broken fingers made of poems.

:::

My grandmother, the mother of my father, loved flowers. Every time I visited her at Khwaza Street I would come back home to Ferguson Road with flowers. I hadn't known that gardens came with plant language... because I didn't know their language, I couldn't speak with them. I went back, to learn their language from the nursery school of my grandmother. She gave me a piece of cloth and a spray bottle full of pure water, and said, Go and dust them, and sing for them while you are working on their leaves.

:::

It is Thursday, maybe the Thursday that Vallejo speaks about… We gathered around the table for good poems, such influence, poetry on a Thursday. We grew like flowers watered by poems, soft voices dancing on our eardrums. David, do you remember how we killed a loaf of brown bread with bananas, really poets are more gentle than thorns. The strelitzia that Maserame fell in love with… I'm here beside a sunflower with a homemade watering can of an old coffee tin.

:::

Day by day the mealie grew taller, as if it was about to meet Jesus Christ very soon. The first day it saw the sun, it wore its green robe to preach love in the garden. At first it was lean and very poor with empty pockets, but one morning it became richer. All its pockets had a cob. It gave me three cobs with their brown-red hair.

Printed in the United States
By Bookmasters